Ali Raheem

Preformace study of WiMAX Network Security

Security Network

GRIN Publishing

Bibliographic information published by the German National Library:

The German National Library lists this publication in the National Bibliography; detailed bibliographic data are available on the Internet at http://dnb.dnb.de .

Imprint:

Copyright © 2011 GRIN Verlag GmbH
Print and binding: Books on Demand GmbH, Norderstedt Germany
ISBN: 978-3-656-28326-3

This book at GRIN:

http://www.grin.com/en/e-book/200705/preformace-study-of-wimax-network-security

GRIN - Your knowledge has value

Since its foundation in 1998, GRIN has specialized in publishing academic texts by students, college teachers and other academics as e-book and printed book. The website www.grin.com is an ideal platform for presenting term papers, final papers, scientific essays, dissertations and specialist books.

Visit us on the internet:

http://www.grin.com/

http://www.facebook.com/grincom

http://www.twitter.com/grin_com

Middlesex
University

MIDDLESEX UNIVERSITY
School of Engineering and Information Sciences

PERFORMACE STUDY OF WiMAX
NETWORK SECURITY

Done By:

Ali Hussein Raheem

CONTENTS:

ABSTRACT: 3

1. INTRODUCTION: 3

2. WIMAX VS WI-FI 6

3. EVAALUATION WIMAX SECURITY: 8

4. WIMAX SOLTTION SECURITY AND IMROVEMENT: 13

5. CONCLUSION: 16

6. REFERENCES... 18

ABSTRACT:

Undeniably, networks have become very important techniques of exchanging information (data) in fast ways. (WIMAX) World Interoperability for Microwave Access is one of the greatest technologies in the communication area. WIMAX has been used widely in telecommunication for long distance communication. From this point, this paper will explore four important sections related to this technique. Firstly, it will discuss the performance conduct of the WIMAX as compared to that of Wi-Fi. Secondly, it will critically evaluate the current solutions for the security problems in WIMAX network. Thirdly, it will attempt to design a new method to improve the security performance of WIMAX network. Fourthly, it will provide a security system that can be applied in real life applications to support the security performance of WIMAX network.

1. INTRODUCTION:

Obviously, using networks techniques has increased especially for the last ten years because of the immense need for data and for communication terms. To begin with, there are different types of network services such as PAN, LAN and WAN. In 2001, a new technology was introduced to our world .i.e the World Interoperability for Microwave Access (WiMAX). WiMAX is the next generation of the wireless technology. It provides high speed mobile to access World Wide Web by using different devices such as notebook PCs and smart phones. As a matter of fact, WiMAX is similar to the fourth generation (4G) of wireless technology. However, it consumes a low cost because it delivers open network and IP mobile to scalable networks data (information). The WiMAX is based on IEEE 802.16 technology and it has developed a third part which is called Fixed WiMAX that is based on the IEEE 802.16d. Unfortunately, the IEEE 802.16d has some real problems resultants of the amendments that have been done to produce the new standard i.e. the IEEE 802.16e that can provide some good features for mobile WiMAX. Figure (1) shows WiMAX network which can be used with different devices .The WiMAX and theWi-Fi can be interoperable to make a large network of communication. [9]

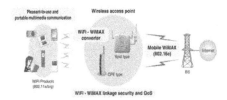

Figure 1: WiMAX Networks [20]

WiMAX can serve as a connection to the public wireless network. It uses optical fiber, microwave link cable or any other elevated speed connectivity. Furthermore, WiMAX uses point to point antennas which join subscriber stations in long distance. Moreover, WiMAX base stations serve many subscriber stations by using Non line of Sight (NLOS) or LOS Point to Multi point connectivity, which could be used both in wired or wireless LAN. Figure 2 shows the way WiMAX works .It is similar to the cell phone where the user sends and receives data that is called uplink and downlink respectively. WiMAX base station has higher broadcasting power which allows sending and receiving data in long distance. When users want to send data (information) from one or different location, the data will be transferred from one cell to another until the data is received.[2]

Figure 2- How WiMAX works [22]

Therefore, when the signal transmits from one location to others, it may cause some attenuation and multi path such as reflection and refraction which will in turn affect the quality of the signal. However, by using orthogonal frequency division multiplexed access (OFDMA) with WIMAX technology, this problem can be solved. WiMAX supports OFDM, which is actually the relation between transmission schemes that are based on the concept of dividing a given high bit rate data stream to several parallel lower bit rate modulations in which every stream has separate carriers which are called subcarriers. In this sense, OFDM is like a spectrally efficient version of multicarrier modulation which is used to limit intermarried interference. Figure 3 shows the benefit of OFDMA. [8]

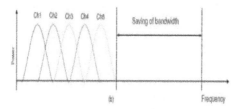

Figure 3: OFDMA [8]

OFDMA has in fact several advantages:[8]

- The OFDMA uses a mixture of both FDMA and TDMA.
- OFDMA is a flexible multiple access technique.
- OFDMA uses the same power of the sending data rate.
- OFDMA minimizes the interface of neighboring cells by using the dissimilar carrier in the cellular system.
- OFDMA decreases the transmitted power and also it dissolves the peak to an average power ratio.

Figure 4 shows WiMAX radio channel which can be either single or multiple carriers. Also, it displays the bandwidth of Wimax radio channel from 1.25 MHz to 28 MHz.

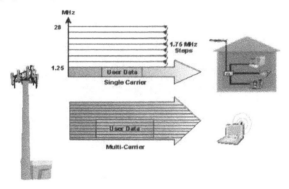

Figure 4: WIMAX radio channel [8]

As a matter of fact, there are two types of WiMAX technology 802.16. Firstly, the Fixed WiMAX which is based on the IEEE 802.16 standards and is actually a fixed broadband service in the sense that it can be either DSL or cable modem service. Secondly, the Mobile WiMAX which is based on the IEEE 802.16e standards .Therefore, it is in fact a combination of both the fixed and the mobile applications that can provide a good performance of security for using mobility. Needless to say, no system is perfect, and WiMAX has some vulnerabilities in its security. The fourth section will therefore tackle and discuss related issues. First, it will discuss the performance analysis of WiMAX as compared to Wi-Fi. Second, it will evaluate current solutions for the security problems in WiMAX network. Third, it will attempt to suggest new design solutions to improve the security performance in WiMAX network. Fourth, it will try to provide a system which can maximize the efficiency of WiMAX security performance. [5][3]

5

2. WiMAX Vs Wi-Fi

Wi-Fi is a wireless technique used for commutation and exchanging of information between the users. In addition, it allows the user to connect different devices such as phone, computers and any other devices that have wireless connection. This technology can be used at home or university without a need to any wired network connection. Wi-Fi network works by using radio technology 802.11 and 2.4 and 5 GHz radio bands. Furthermore, the coverage area of Wi-Fi ranges from 10meter to 2 km. Figure 4 shows the Wi-Fi network which can connect different devices.

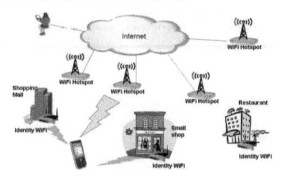

Figure 5: Wi-Fi network [20]

There are different generations of Wi-Fi [18][19]

- Wi-Fi 802.11a which has frequency band 5 and transfer data (Bandwidth) 54 Mbps.
- Wi-Fi technology 802.11b which has frequency band 5 GHz and maximum data rate 11.
- Wi-Fi 802.11g which has frequency 2.4-5 GHz and bandwidth 450 Mbps.

Each generation has different frequencies and bandwidths but all of them can work together. The advantages of Wi-Fi can be summarized as the following:

- It uses unlicensed portion of spectrum and does not need many controls for many countries.
- Wi-Fi does not need any physical cables for connection.
- Wi-Fi is very cheap and many products of Wi-Fi are available in the market.
- Wi-Fi is fast in transferring the data in short distances.

As for the disadvantages of Wi-Fi, they are the following:

6

- The 802.11g and 802.11 standards of the Wi-Fi use 2.4 GHZ spectrum, which can cause problems to other devices such as microwave ovens and cordless phones . It could affect and degrade the performance of these devices.
- Sometimes, it wastes power. It can shorten and limit the range of home router using 802.1b or 802.1g while it has a range of 46m indoors and 92 outdoors.
- Wi-Fi is not a good technique for transferring the data in long distances.

Wi-Fi has some problems in security with WEP and WPA1 techniques; therefore, it uses now WPA2 which provides duplex security.

However, WiMAX has more properties than Wi-Fi; for example, WiMAX provides further long distances range than the Wi-Fi. On the other hand, the WiMAX is not good for transferring a data in short distances. [1][2]

WiMAX has different advantages:

- A single station in WiMAX can serve many users at the same time.
- WiMAX is much faster than other networks and does not need a wire for connection.
- WiMAX provides high speed and it can reach 10 MPS at 10 Kilometers with line site.

As for the disadvantages, here are some:

- The line site in WiMAX is required for longer connections.
- The weather conditions such as rains and storms can affect the signal of the WiMAX.
- Using other wireless equipments could cause interference to signal.
- WiMAX needs much power, which causes in turn wasting the power supply.
- WiMAX needs a big installation and operation system which is often so costly.

Figure 5 shows the WiMAX network which can serve different users at the same time and from different long distances.

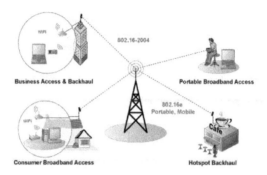

Figure 5: WiMAX Network [21]

3. EVAALUATION WiMAX SECURITY:

In this part, WiMAX security will be discussed to have a clear overview of WiMAX network. WiMAX uses encryption which is a mechanism that provides secured data called data confidentiality and integrity. Furthermore, WiMAX uses the encryption which means taking the plaintext and mixing the data (information) by applying a complex mathematical algorithm to produce cipher text. The cipher text is transmitted over the wireless network and cannot be understood by the hacker who wants to steal the information. Figure 6 shows WiMAX Advanced Encryption Standard (AES) which is used to create cipher text .The latter can protect the information from any attack that could happen at any moment. Furthermore, AES takes encryption key and uses a counter one as an input to produce and create a bit stream. Finally, the bit stream will be XOR with the plaintext to create the Cipher text as Figure 6 shows. When the receiver receives the data (information), it will reverse this process to recover the plaintext. However, to activate this process, the transmitter and receiver should use the same encryption key. [10]

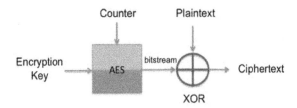

Figure 6: AES Encryption [12]

Moreover, WiMAX uses public key infrastructure and the 802.16e standard of WiMAX that uses version 2 which is (PKMv2). This version provides a good privacy and key management protocol.[5] In addition, PKMv2 provides data security specially when transferring the key between the base station and mobile station. Also, this version identifies the users and whether the data is valid or not. Furthermore, it provides an authorization key (AK) which is very important to obtain the encryption key. The PKMv2 uses the Rivest Shamir Adlerman (RSA) which is the public key cryptography exchange. Therefore, RSA public key requires identity from the mobile station, which can be the X.509 digital certificate, or uses immediately the subscriber identity module (SIM) card. The X.509 digital certificate contains the MAC address, which the certificate uses for authority. Figure (7) shows the certificate authority that validates the certificate that can identify the user. When the user identity is validated, the WiMAX network uses the public key to generate authorization key and transmit it to the mobile station.[13][19]

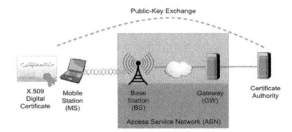

Figure 7: Public key infrastructure in WiMAX [12]

WiMAX uses an Extensible Authentication Protocol (EAP) which is used to check the user authentication before accessing to the network. Furthermore, the EAP is the authentication framework which is used to perform the user authentication. Figure (8) shows the authentication process to identify and validate the user .i.e. whether he belongs to this service or not. It shows also that the messages can be defined by using the EAP

9

method and can be then transmitted to the mobile station for the authenticator. Subsequently, the authenticator forwards the messages to the authentication server by using the RADIUS or DIAMETER protocols.[18][7]

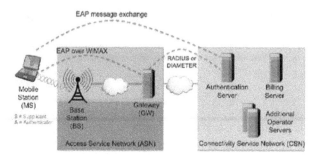

Figure 8: the EAP based authentication WiMAX [12]

Also, the EAP is used to exchange and validate the user, as figure (8) shows, to allow the user get access control. It is possible therefore to say that this process looks similar to the authenticate users in Wi-Fi network.

On the other hand, the authentication mechanism that is used in WiMAX and that follows the privacy and the key management (PKM) protocol has some weaknesses in the base station (BS) that provides the authentication itself. This causes Man-in-the-Middle Attacks issue, which can affect and expose the confidentiality information of the subscribers. Another problem in WiMAX is the encryption that has been mentioned in the previous part. 802.16e supports the AES cipher which means that the data is more secure. But unfortunately, the management frames are not encrypted in the 802.11 which means that they are more liable to be exposed to attackers and hackers. WiMAX uses licensed RF spectrum, which gives the network a kind of protection against unintentional interference. On the other hand, attackers use different tools to break the spectrum for all planned WiMAX. Furthermore, when the physical denial of services is attacked by hacker, this attacker can use many management frames which can cause the disconnection of stations. [13]

Based on this, there are many attacks that can threat WiMAX security and as the following:[1]

- Rogue Base Stations
- Dos Attacks
- Man-in-the-Middle Attacks

- Network manipulation of spoofed management frames

Man-in-the-Middle Attack is one of the many problems faced by WiMAX security .This is because the attacker (hacker) can steal the messages or the information through the process of communication or public key exchange .He/she can also change this information and transmit it to the original user. Accordingly, this part will consider the analysis of Point to Multi-Point (PMP) topology. The PMP mode is the most important side in the BS; it is the central node that connects the users to the network. Also, it allocates the radio resources for the SS, and these resources are the Downlink and Uplink that use different frequencies or time slots. Therefore, Base Station has the ability to use the downlink channel in the same way Subscriber Station has the ability to use the Uplink channel. Figure (9) shows the procedures of initializing a network which are considered as the most significant security operation in the Mobile WiMAX .This is because it contains many different processes. To initial ranging processes, the SS Basic Capability (SBC) is a negotiation process, PKM is authentication process .And finally, Ranging Request (RNG-REQ) and Ranging Response (RNG-RSP) are registration process.[19]

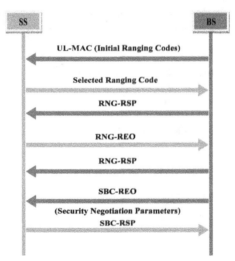

Figure 9: The Initial network entry process

Unfortunately, the mobile WiMAX standard does not provide good security mechanism that can keep the SBC negotiation information secret. This is because there are possibilities of intercepting or capturing the messages at the same time the entry process is going on .Through such intervention, the contents of the messages can be even changed. Figure (10) shows that the attacker can identify himself as the original SS and

11

send tamped SBCRSP messages to the serving BS. In brief, the attacker then can damage, steal or change all the information in these messages. The contact or the communication between the SS and BS will not be encrypted. Consequently this means that the system is a failure.[1]

wiretap and tamper all the information transmitted.

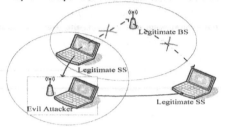

Figure 10: Attack (RNG-RSP DOS) [15]

However, the Denial of service (DOS) causes some risks in WiMAX security. In the initial network, the Ranging Request (RNG-REQ) message can be sent from the SS to the BS to join the network, and then the message will be processed. The BS has the ability to respond to the SS by using the Ranging Response (RNG-RSP) which contains all the information. Unfortunately, the RNG-RSP message will not be encrypted and hence will not be authenticated. This means that the attacker (hacker) will take this as an advantage to hack the information (data). For instance, hackers could change the message from RNG-RSP, and then when the BS receives the message from the victim, SS aborts all transmission and reinstalls its MAC. Figure (11) shows this attack: [17][18]

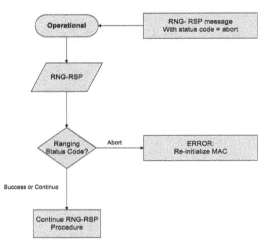

Figure 11: RNG –RSP DOS attack

4. WiMAX SOLTTION SECURITY AND IMROVEMENT:

The previous section has tested the Man in the Middle Attacks and the DOS attacks issue through the mobile WiMAX. These two types of attacks can be limited and stopped by using a new security technique which is referred to as SINEP. SINEP is an advanced technique that is used to achieve a secure connection with the network, .i.e. the network security can be provided by the authentication and the key negotiation. A lot of important information can be exchanged through these procedures. Although there are no reliable and appropriate methods to protect these messages against disposal security weaknesses during the initial network entry, SINEP has been greatly recommended .The latter is based on the Diffie- Hellman (DH) key exchange protocol. The DH agreement is a key management method which can exchange or share encryption key with the global change variables known as prime number "p" and 'r' where "r" is the primitive root of p. [13]Furthermore, the DH key is an exchange protocol and it is described as shown in figure (12).

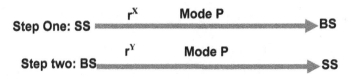

Figure 12: Diffile –Hellman (HD) key exchange protocol

13

However, X is the private key which belongs to the Subscriber Station, and Y belongs to the key of the Base Station. SS public key can be represented by $PK_{SS} = r^X$ mode p, and BS public key can be represented by $PK_{BS} = r^Y$ mode P. Therefore, both of the SS and BS can derive the same shared private key by using the following equation as figure (13) shows:

$$K_{share} = (PK_{bs})^X \text{mode } p = (r^Y \text{mode } p)^X \text{mode } p$$

$$= r^{YX} \text{mod } p = (r^{xy})^Y \text{mod } p$$

$$= (r^{YX} \text{mode } p)^Y \text{mod } p$$

$$= (PK_{ss})^Y \text{mode } p$$

Figure 13: Derive Equation

After performing the above mentioned procedures, the SS and the BS can share the same private key which is K_{share}. The Dos attacks during the initial network entry process can be stopped by the DH key. Also, by using the shared private key which is K_{shar} the message can be encrypted. Never the less, this system or process cannot prevent the Man in the Middle Attack from attacking the network because these procedures do not provide the identity authentication. Figure (14) shows how Man in the Middle Attack happens.

$$\text{step one: } SS \xrightarrow{r^X \text{ mod } p} ES$$
$$\text{step two: } ES \xrightarrow{r^Z \text{ mod } p} BS$$
$$\text{step three: } BS \xrightarrow{r^Y \text{ mod } p} ES$$
$$\text{step four: } ES \xrightarrow{r^Z \text{ mod } p} SS$$

Figure 14: Man in the middle attack toward HD

AS figure 14 shows, the victim SS has the public key which is PK_{SS} that can be attacked by the Evil station (ES). In addition, the ES hiding as the SS sends its own public key PKES to BS. Therefore, the BS will send back the key which is PKBS. Simultaneously,

14

the ES could share this key with the BS. In the end, the Evil Station (E S) will send its own public key PKES to the victim SS. So ES will share the key with the SS and all the messages between the SS and BS can be read by the ES who can even change the content of these messages. To oppose or stop the Man in the Middle Attacks in this situation, it is necessary to improve the DH key exchange protocol by providing an identity authentication. It is quiet important to make first a kind of simple announcement which is similar to a one way function that can generate a hash value x, for example, by using a//b which means that a//b is a cascaded. Furthermore, by supposing that every SS has its own international Subscriber Station Identity |ISSI| and by using |SS|, the SS has the ability to generate a Temporary Subscriber Station Identity (TSSI) .In this manner, TSSI is being used in the protocol as the SS identity. Then, let us suppose that legitimate BS has a hash value, the H (TSSI) is generated by the SS TSSI. By using the H (TSSI) as an input, parameter of the hash authentication functions as an alternative of using TSSI, because in a particular situation one of legitimate BSs maybe captured from the attacker. On the other hand, the storing H (TSSI) in the BS stops the attackers to reach the SS TSSI. There are five important steps in our protocol:

1. SS imitates the legitimate user.
2. BS transmits a random number which can be represented by R_{BS} as challenge to SS.
3. SS has the responsibility of calculating H (TSSI). Then it cascades H (TSSI), R_{BS} and its public key PK_{SS} to be as inputs to generate the response for BS challenge, $H(TSSI)\|R_{BS} \| PK_{SS})$. Finally, SS sends the response: its public key and its challenge, R_{SS} to BS.
4. The BS calculates the hash value by using the stored $H(TTSI)$, the R_{BS} and PK_{SS} as inputs and compares it with the SS reply which is used to check whether the SS is legitimate or not. If not the BS will stop the communication otherwise the BS calculates the hash value by using the following equation H $(TSSI\|R_{SS}\|PK_{BS})$; after that, the Bs will send the hash value and its own public key to SS.
5. The SS will check the BS identity by using the response it received, so if the BS is legitimate, the shared key will recognize the SS and will then establish the communication with the BS .Otherwise ,it will cut-off the connection.

SINEP has been developed by using the enhanced DH key exchange. Figure 15 shows the secure initial network entry:

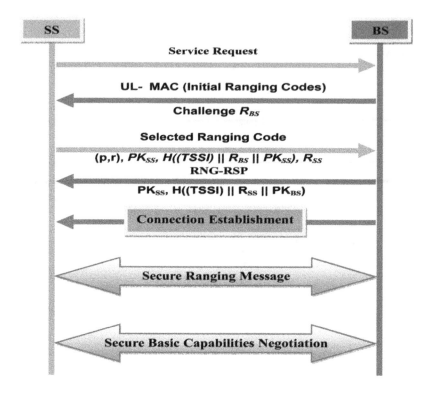

Figure 15: SINEP Scheme

SINEP has successfully stopped and resisted both types of attacks namely the Dos and Man-in-the-Middle Attacks since the authentication is achieved. Furthermore, by this protocol, the SS can share the private key with the BS and this key will be used as an encryption.

5. CONCLUSION:

After taking everything into consideration, WiMAX is a new technology that is being used for communication requirements. By using WiMAX, a wide area can be covered in a way that allows many users to communicate or exchange the information with each other. In this is paper, an overview has been given about how WiMAX works. Also this paper has compared WiMAX with the Wi-Fi network and has also showed that both of these networks have advantages and disadvantages. The focus of this paper was on the issues of security in WiMAX, and it has been discovered that there are different attacks that could affect the performance of WiMAX network and its security. A solution has been suggested which is developing the SINEP to stop and limit these attacks .In this way; we can change and maximize the performance of security in WiMAX to a high level.

6. REFERENCES

[1]"Mobile WiMAX security", Airspan Networks Inc. 2007.. Available Online: http://www.airspan.com D. Johnston and J. Walker, "Overview of IEEE 802.16 security", *IEEE Security Privacy,* vol. 2, no. 3, pp. 40-48, Accessed (1-4-2010)

[2]F. Yang and J. Feng. "An improved security scheme in WiMAX based on IEEE standard 802.16", in 2005 International Conference on Wireless Communications, Networking and Mobile Computing, Accessed (1-4-2010)

[3] C.-T. Huang, "Security issues in privacy and key management protocols of IEEE WiMAX 802.16," in ACM Southeast Regional Conference, R.Menezes, Ed. ACM, 2006, pp. 113-118. Access (1-4-2010)

[4]Datta A., He C. and Mitchell J.C., "802.16e Notes," Stanford University, CA, USA, 2005. Available Online: http://www.iab.org/liaisons/ieee/EAP/802.16eNotes.pdf . Access (4-4-2010)

[5]Yuksel E., "Analysis of the PKMv2 Protocol in IEEE WiMAX 802.16e-2005 Using Static Analysis Informatics and Mathematical Modeling", TUD, 2007. Available Online: http://www2.imm.dtu.dk/pubdb/views/publication_details.ph Access (4-4-2010)

[6]Ju-Yi Kuo, "Analysis of 802.16e Multicast /Broadcast group privacy rekeying protocol" , Stanford University, CA,USA, 2006.Available Online: http://www.stanford.edu/ Access (4-4-2010)

[7]Wook Choi, "An Analysis of Mobile WiMAX Security: Vulnerabilities and Solutions", *Lecture Notes in Computer Science,* vol. 4658, pp. 88-97, Aug. 2007. Accessed (5-4-2010)

[8]Ramjee Prasad *"OFDM for Wireless Multimedia Communication"* Artech House Publishers, 2000.Accessed (5-4-2010)

[9]Bing Xie; Jun-de Song, *"Link-level Simulation and Performance Estimation IEEE WiMAX 802.16e",* 2nd International Conference on Pervasive Computing and Applications, Page(s):667 – 671, Accessed (5-4-2010)

[10]Griffin "Creating a Secure Network for Your Business", White-Paper, 2005. http://www.aometrosystems.com/whitepaper.htm Accessed (5-4-2010)

[11]Westech Communication Inc (2006), *Can WiMAX Address Your Application*, White Paper, and Accessed (6-4-2010).

[12]C.T. Huang, Security issues in privacy and key management protocols of IEEE WiMAX 802.16, in *Proceedings of ACM SE'06.* Accessed (6-4-2010)

[13]J. Walker, "Overview of IEEE WiMAX 802.16 security", *IEEE Security and Privacy*, pp. 40–48, Accessed (7-4-2010)

[14]S.B. Wang, "Efficient certificate less authentication and key agreement (CL-AK) for Grid computing, "International Journal of Network Security, Vol.7, No.3, 2008,pp.342–347. Accessed (7-4-2010)

[15]J.H Li, "Two-party authenticated key agreement in certificate less public key cryptography," Wuhan University Journal of Natural Sciences, Vol. 12(1), 2007, pp. 71-74. Accessed (8-4-2010)

[16]T.K. Mandt, "Certificateless authenticated two-party key agreement protocols," In Advances in Computer Science -ASIAN 2007, Secure Software and Related Issues, Springer Berlin / Heidelberg, Vol. 4435 of Lecture Notes in Computer Science, 2008, pp. 37-44, Accessed (8-4-2010)

[17]T. ElGamal, "A public key cryptosystem and signature scheme based on discrete logarithms," IEEE Transactions on Information Theory, Vol.31, 1985, pp. 469-472, doi: 10.1007/3-540-39568-7. Accessed (8-4-2010)

[18]A. Arkoudi-Vafea, "Security of IEEE WiMAX 802.16.Master of Information and Communication Systems Security," Department of Computer and Systems–Science Royal Institute of Technology, 2007. Accessed (8-4-2010)

[19]S. Wattanachai, "Security Architecture of the IEEE WiMAX 802.16 Standard for Mesh Networks," Department of Computer and Systems Sciences Stockholm University/Royal Institute of Technology,2007.Accessed (8-4-2010)

[20] Wi-Fi Security, how to secure your Wi-Fi network, available online, http://www.aboutonlinetips.com/wi-fi-security-how-to-secure-your-wi-fi-network/ , Accessed (8-4-2010)

[21] 4G, WiMAX, available online, http://www.yugatech.com/blog/telecoms/why-is-4gwimax-in-the-philippines-slow/ , Accessed (8-4-2010)

[22] WiMAX, available online, http://library.thinkquest.org Accessed (8-4-2010)